AN AD
throug

God
with Us
IMMANUEL

Carol Tetzlaff
managing editor

REDEMPTION PRESS

God with Us

IMMANUEL

© 2024 by Carol Tetzlaff. All rights reserved.

Published by Redemption Press, 1602 Cole Street, Enumclaw, WA 98022, (360) 226-3488.

Redemption Press is honored to present this title in partnership with the author. The views expressed or implied in this work are those of the author. Redemption Press provides our imprint seal representing design excellence, creative content, and high-quality production.

Noncommercial interests may reproduce portions of this book without the express written permission of the author, provided the text does not exceed five hundred words. When reproducing text from this book, include the following credit line: "*God with Us, Immanuel*, by Carol Tetzlaff. Used by permission."

Commercial interests: No part of this publication may be reproduced in any form, stored in a retrieval system, or transmitted in any form by any means—electronic, photocopy, recording, or otherwise—without prior written permission of the publisher/author, except as provided by United States of America copyright law.

Unless otherwise indicated, all Scripture quotations are taken from The Holy Bible, New International Version® NIV®, Copyright © 1973, 1978, 1984, 2011 by Biblica, Inc.Used with permission. All rights reserved worldwide.

Scripture quotations marked NLT are taken from the Holy Bible, New Living Translation, copyright © 1996, 2004, 2015 by Tyndale House Foundation. Used by permission of Tyndale House Publishers, Inc., Carol Stream, Illinois 60188. All rights reserved.

Scripture quotations marked ESV are from the ESV® Bible (The Holy Bible, English Standard Version®), © 2001 by Crossway, a publishing ministry of Good News Publishers. Used by permission. All rights reserved. The ESV text may not be quoted in any publication made available to the public by a Creative Commons license. The ESV may not be translated in whole or in part into any other language.

Scripture quotations marked AMP are taken from the Amplified® Bible (AMP), Copyright © 2015 by The Lockman Foundation. Used by permission. lockman.org

Scriptures marked NKJV taken from the New King James Version®. Copyright © 1982 by Thomas Nelson. Used by permission. All rights reserved.

Scripture quotations marked NASB taken from the (NASB®) New American Standard Bible®, Copyright © 1960, 1971, 1977, 1995, 2020 by The Lockman Foundation. Used by permission. All rights reserved. lockman.org

Scripture quotations marked CSB have been taken from the Christian Standard Bible®, Copyright © 2017 by Holman Bible Publishers. Used by permission. Christian Standard Bible® and CSB® are federally registered trademarks of Holman Bible Publishers.

Scripture quotations marked GNT are from the Good News Translation in Today's English Version-Second Edition Copyright © 1992 by American Bible Society. Used by Permission.

Scripture quotations marked (KJV) are taken from the King James Version, public domain.

Scriptures marked (MEV) taken from the Modern English Version. Copyright © 2014 by Military Bible Association. Used by permission. All rights reserved.

Scripture quotations marked MSG are taken from THE MESSAGE, copyright © 1993, 2002, 2018 by Eugene H. Peterson. Used by permission of NavPress. All rights reserved. Represented by Tyndale House Publishers, Inc.

ISBN 13: 978-1-64645-233-0

Library of Congress Catalog Card

*May the God of hope
fill you with all joy
and peace as you trust in him,
so that you may overflow with hope
by the power of the Holy Spirit.*
Romans 15:13 NIV

God is love.
I John 4:8 NLT

Contents

Introduction	1
The Genealogy of Jesus	3
Advent HOPE	**5**
DAY 1	The With of God	Carol Tetzlaff	7
DAY 2	God with Adam	Angela Mackey	11
DAY 3	God with Seth	Faith Blum	15
DAY 4	God with Enoch	Jerri Lien	19
DAY 5	God with Methuselah	Cherie Fletcher	23
DAY 6	God with Noah	Tracy Harper	27
DAY 7	God with Abraham	Claire Alameda	31
Advent PEACE	**35**
DAY 8	God with Isaac	Carolyn Dale Newell	37
DAY 9	God with Jacob	Janet Johnson	41
DAY 10	God with Judah	Marsha Price	45
*Bonus	God with Tamar	Kathy Watson-Swift*	49
DAY 11	God with Perez	Joy Wendling	53
DAY 12	God with Salmon	Chantel Mathson	57
*Bonus	God with Rahab	Athena Dean Holtz*	61
DAY 13	God with Boaz	Susan Perelka	65
*Bonus	God with Ruth	Elizabeth Abshire*	69
DAY 14	God with Jesse	Sandi Banks	73

Advent JOY 77

DAY 15 | God with David | Sherri Cullison 79

Bonus | God with Bathsheba | Bethany Widmer 83

DAY 16 | God with Solomon | Tracey Druyor 87

DAY 17 | God with Rehoboam | Lori May 91

DAY 18 | God with Abijah | Gayla Campbell 95

DAY 19 | God with Asa | Page Gyatt 99

DAY 20 | God with Jehosaphat | Liz Holtzman 101

DAY 21 | God with Uzziah | Jackie Freeman 105

Advent LOVE 109

DAY 22 | God with Ahaz | Elizabeth Renicks 111

DAY 23 | God with Hezekiah | Shelly Brown 115

DAY 24 | God with Josiah | Crystal Manget 119

DAY 25 | God with Jeconiah | Janell Neumann 123

DAY 26 | God with Zerubbabel | Sara Beekman 127

DAY 27 | God with Joseph | Marie Palecek 131

Bonus | God with Mary (mother of Jesus) | Leasha Rutschman 135

Advent JESUS 139

DAY 28 | God with Jesus | Maureen Wild 141

Compilation Authors 145

Introduction

Advent is a season of celebration. Twenty-eight days to lean in and remember the promised Messiah. Themes of hope, peace, joy, and love bring us to a manger, and there we find Jesus.

The storyline found in the genealogies of Jesus in Matthew 1 and Luke 3 give us entrance into the miraculous scene. The promise of Jesus when time began ushered in by God Himself.

On the pages of this devotional, you will embark on a journey that begins with God, in the beginning. He is present with His creation. Man fails miserably and sin plagues this narrative, yet God is still there. Our encounter with each of these characters enters us into a race toward the moment when man would once again be found in the presence of God. Jesus would come and make His dwelling among men. Immanuel, God wraps Himself and flesh and lives among men.

This journey includes twenty-eight days of readings beginning at creation and ending at the manger. The themes of Advent are evident as God ushers in hope, peace, joy, and love through the promise of His Son.

Five women are mentioned in the genealogy of Jesus found in Matthew 1. These devotions will be a bonus entry as we recognize the value God placed upon women to carry the seed of the Messiah.

The Christmas season will bring you into the story of Jesus as you engage in these pages. Do it alone, around the table with your family, or with a group. To receive additional resources and discussion questions to guide you through this devotional during Advent, scan the QR code.

The Genealogy of Jesus

The verses included are those featured in this devotional.

Matthew 1:1–17 NLT

This is a record of the ancestors of Jesus the Messiah,
a descendant of David and of Abraham:
² Abraham was the father of Isaac.
Isaac was the father of Jacob.
Jacob was the father of Judah and his brothers
³ Judah was the father of Perez ... (whose mother was Tamar)

...

⁵ Salmon was the father of Boaz (whose mother was Rahab).
Boaz was the father of Obed (whose mother was Ruth).
Obed was the father of Jesse.
⁶ Jesse was the father of King David.
David was the father of Solomon
(whose mother was Bathsheba, the widow of Uriah).
⁷ Solomon was the father of Rehoboam.
Rehoboam was the father of Abijah.
Abijah was the father of Asa.
⁸ Asa was the father of Jehoshaphat.

...

⁹ Uzziah was the father of Jotham.
Jotham was the father of Ahaz.
Ahaz was the father of Hezekiah.

...

¹¹ Josiah was the father of Jehoiachin and his brothers
(born at the time of the exile to Babylon).
¹² After the Babylonian exile:

Jehoiachin was the father of Shealtiel.
Shealtiel was the father of Zerubbabel.

...

16 Jacob was the father of Joseph, the husband of Mary.
Mary gave birth to Jesus, who is called the Messiah.
17 All those listed above include fourteen generations from Abraham to David, fourteen from David to the Babylonian exile, and fourteen from the Babylonian exile to the Messiah.

Luke 3:23–38 NLT

23 Jesus was about thirty years old when he began his public ministry.
Jesus was known as the son of Joseph.]

...

Zerubbabel was the son of Shealtiel.

...

32 David was the son of Jesse.
Jesse was the son of Obed.
Obed was the son of Boaz.
Boaz was the son of Salmon.

...

Perez was the son of Judah.
34 Judah was the son of Jacob.
Jacob was the son of Isaac.
Isaac was the son of Abraham.
Abraham was the son of Terah.

...

Shem was the son of Noah.

...

Methuselah was the son of Enoch.

...

Seth was the son of Adam.
Adam was the son of God.

HOPE Week One

Believers embrace hope differently than the world. Our hope is grounded in confident faith within the promises of God.

> *Faith shows the reality of what we hope for;*
> *it is the evidence of things we cannot see.*
> Hebrews 11:1 NLT

As you enter this first week of Advent, may you find hope in the promise that is to come. God ushers in the beginning of time and engages within the narrative of His creation.

~ *Prayer* ~

God Almighty, as I enter this week,
I set my eyes on all that you have for me.
Through those who sinned and those who followed faithfully,
may I see myself, and may my faith be strengthened in hope
with full assurance you will keep your promises.
I will look for You and find You are with me.
Amen

To receive additional resources and discussion questions to guide you through this devotional during Advent, scan the QR code.

The With of God

DAY 1

In the beginning God ...
Genesis 1:1 ESV

Eternal, no beginning or ending, the first and the last, Alpha, Omega ... this is our God. Always known, yet He created time and space for man to know Him.

Elohim entered Himself into our story through the pages of His Word. We read the creation scene ushering in His presence to a world shaped by the sound of his voice: *Let there be ...* and *it is good.*

The grand finale, man, is formed by the hands of the Almighty, and his first breath encounters the everlasting God. This scene sweeps man into God's presence! God with man and man with God.

Life in the garden was good until it was not. The sin of man burrowed a chasm between them as man hid from

God, placing Him at a distance. Yet God never moved; man did. The steps their Creator would take to bring them back with Him were drastic, for one of God's precious created beasts would shed its own blood.

Their relationship was restored, yet man would live in the harsh realities of the world engulfed in sin and longing to realize His presence.

Throughout the narrative of Scripture, we see God present with His creation as they come to know Him and experience Him in their lives. Sin launched a promise of complete reconciliation with God as mankind would carry the seed of the Messiah.

The very *with* of God walked with man in the beginning, and Immanuel, God with us, would enter the world to fulfill the promise.

The With of God

Practice

Do you know the *with* of God in your life?
What separates you from His presence?
Confess and be restored.

Prayer

God Almighty, You are with me!
As I enter this season of Advent,
may I be with You and drawn into
Your presence. Amen.

Promise

The Word became flesh and made his dwelling among us.
We have seen his glory, the glory of the one and only Son,
who came from the Father, full of grace and truth.
John 1:14 NIV

~ Carol Tetzlaff

God With Us

God with Adam

DAY 2

So the LORD God banished him from the Garden of Eden to work the ground from which he had been taken.
Genesis 3:23 NIV

Everything was ruined. One bite of the fruit that promised wisdom, and I knew. I was naked. Was the weight in my chest shame or fear? Nothing was the same; somehow the very earth beneath my feet felt different. Was it an undoing or an estrangement?

Eve, the woman I delighted in, seemed a stranger. It was her fault. She took the fruit; I just took a bite because she did. Now naked and desperate, we sit sewing leaves to cover our shame because we know He will be coming. I used to look forward to walking with Him, but now I dread it.

"He's coming!"

"Let's hide!"

***

God came with a question, not condemnation. He came with justice and grace. He told Adam and Eve the consequences of their choices. The breaking of relational wholeness, the pain of childbirth, and the sweat and toil that would be required to bring forth fruit. Then God banished them from the garden, where the tree of knowledge stood alongside the tree of life.

God could have struck Adam and Eve dead when they ate of the tree of the knowledge of good and evil. He could have let them stay in the garden and eat of the tree of life. Then they would live forever separated from God. Instead, He banished them from the garden so they could have a right relationship with Him. He gave a future promise that one day the serpent would be defeated.

He comes to us with the same promise. Our sin does not have the final word. Jesus has paid the penalty for our sin and given us His righteousness. God's kindness draws us to repentance, and He will never leave us. He is with us.

When shame and condemnation try to make us hide, let us listen for God's still small voice. He is calling us home.

Practice

How are you hiding from God?
Confess these things, and allow God to restore
the joy of your salvation.

Prayer

Father God, thank You for calling out to me in kindness.
Help me to lay bare my heart
so I can rejoice in Your presence.

Promise

Where can I go from your Spirit?
Where can I flee from your presence?
If I go up to the heavens, you are there;
if I make my bed in the depths, you are there.
Psalm 139:7–8 NIV

~Angela Mackey

God With Us

God with Seth

DAY 3

And Adam knew his wife again, and she bore a son and called his name Seth, *for she said, "God has appointed for me another offspring instead of Abel, for Cain killed him."*
Genesis 4:25 ESV

The labor pains intensified. Adam encouraged Eve to push. Relief came as the baby finally appeared.

"It's a boy!" Adam exclaimed.

Eve reached for her son. "God has appointed for me another offspring instead of Abel." She looked into his sweet, wet face. The wound on her heart healed ever so slightly as she into Seth's eyes. He would never know his older brothers, Cain and Abel, and this thirdborn son would receive all the blessings of the firstborn. "You are a promise from God," she whispered into his tiny ear. Seth cooed, and Eve smiled up at her husband.

God With Us

Not much is said about Seth in the Bible, but he became the catalyst for all of God's promises and in the lineage of Jesus. In Genesis 3:15 (ESV), God promised the serpent, "He [Eve's seed] shall bruise your head, and you shall bruise his heel." Through Seth, this promise was fulfilled many generations later through Jesus.

***

I can relate to Eve. We lost two babies to miscarriage before our son was born. I'm sure when Eve held Seth for the first time, she was thinking of the promise God made in Genesis 3:15. No matter how hard it is—still—to see other pregnant women, I remember God will always do as He promised. Despite the sorrow of losing a loved one—whether miscarriage, infertility, untimely death, or old age—we know that God has a plan, and He will bring us comfort in His own way and timing. For me, that was our son, David. For you it will be something else.

We can all experience God with us as Seth did by trusting God to be the promise keeper, as He has been since the beginning of time.

Practice

How has God fulfilled a promise in your life?

Prayer

Heavenly Father, thank You for Your care for us
and for always being there for us.
We love You and know that You will always
accomplish Your promises.

Promise

Blessed are those who mourn,
for they shall be comforted.
Matthew 5:4 ESV

~Faith Blum

God With Us

God with Enoch

DAY 4

By faith [that pleased God] Enoch was caught up and taken to heaven
so that he would not have a glimpse of death;
and he was not found for God had taken him;
for even before he was taken [to heaven],
he received the testimony [still on record]
that he had walked with God and pleased Him.
Hebrews 11:5 AMP

Marvelously and mysteriously, God took Enoch.

Enoch was a faithful man who walked closely with the Lord and never experienced earthly death. We're given few details of Enoch's life, yet we know he pleased God because of his faith and constant fellowship with Him.

A loving friend longed to hear from God but admitted she never read the Bible. God gave us Scripture so we can know Him. He speaks to us through His Word. My friend was encouraged to begin reading the Bible daily. Once she determined to do so, her faith began flourishing. Her light shines even more brightly in the lives of others because she is spending time with God.

Faith comes by hearing the word of God. When we immerse ourselves in His Word and purposefully fellowship with Him, we too can be people of faith! Reading, memorizing, writing out Scripture, and hearing God's Word being spoken and taught will lead us to become people of faith. Faith in God is what pleases Him.

We cannot perfectly mold and plan our lives, but we can choose to believe God. We can choose to walk daily and have perpetual communication with Him.

God With Enoch

Practice

How is your walk of faith?
Delving into His Word pleases the Father
and draws you closer to Him.
If this feels overwhelming, start by reading daily devotions,
perhaps with a friend or family member.

Prayer

Heavenly Father, Your word shows us those
who pleased You were imperfect,
yet they were people of faith.
May we be people of faith who please You.
We crave your nearness, Father.
Thank You, God, that You are with us
just as You were with Enoch.

Promise

*You will keep in perfect and constant peace
the one whose mind is steadfast
[that is, committed and focused on You—
in both inclination and character],
Because he trusts and takes refuge in You
[with hope and confident expectation].*
Isaiah 26:3 AMP

~Jerri Lien

God With Us

God with Methuselah

DAY 5

*When Methuselah was 187 years old, he had Lamech.
After he had Lamech, he lived another 782 years.
Methuselah lived a total of 969 years.
And he died.*
Genesis 5:25–27 MSG

I cannot imagine living 969 years in this evil world.

Nevertheless, that is what Methuselah did. He lived during a time when humans were so depraved, God regretted that He had made man.

The Bible does not record much more about Methuselah's life. However, a few things intrigue me about him: He was the oldest man who ever lived, his name means *his death sends*, and he died the year of the Flood. Even in the brevity of the narrative of his life, he left a legacy of righteousness in his grandson and perhaps was one of the faithful who helped Noah build the ark.

***

God suffers long with humankind because He desires that none will perish but that all would come to the knowledge of the truth (1 Timothy 2:4). Throughout our lives He teaches, encourages, supports, strengthens, and woos us into alignment with his heart. All He asks is we read His Word, listen to His voice, and obey.

I am living witness that God has not only cared for me but has suffered long through my seventy-six years of ups and downs. Though I was raised in a Christian home, it took me well into my adult life to realize the precepts in God's Word will not only assist and guide me, but will help me become the person He intended.

God With Methuselah

Practice

Are there areas in your life prompting you to ask,
"Where is God in all of this?"
If so, write them down and ask God to help you recognize
where He's being faithful to His Word.

Prayer

Father, as we lay our cares at Your feet,
help us to realize there is nothing too big or too small
for You to handle.
Help us to recognize
that even though things surrounding us
seem to be a little murky,
You are carrying us through it all.

Promise

*You who have been carried by Me from your birth
and have been carried [in My arms] from the womb,
even to your old age I am He,
and even to your advanced old age I will carry you!
I have made you, and I will carry you;
Be assured I will carry you and I will save you.*
Isaiah 46:3–4 AMP

~Cherie K. Fletcher

God With Us

God with Noah

DAY 6

*And those that entered, male and female of all flesh,
went in as God had commanded him.
And the Lord shut him in.*
Genesis 7:16 ESV

Time stands still as one dark day blurs into the next. Noah cannot remember the sun's warmth, solid ground, and pure air untainted by animals.

Months ago, he had found favor with God due to his right character and conduct. In His grace, God saved Noah and his family from the judgment He brought on the earth—a flood that wiped away an increasingly wicked human race. Now, Noah wonders if God has forgotten him. Will the deep floodwaters ever recede? Will he live out the remainder of his days imprisoned by the vessel that initially rescued him?

***

God With Us

We can do all the "right" things in our relationship with God yet be enveloped in darkness. Noah was an obedient man who *walked faithfully with God*.

Unceasing rain pounded the metal roof of our rental home on Hawaii Island. I felt trapped. Panic swelled. We had left our East Coast home to follow God's call to ministry at the most diverse university in the nation with our family and friends far away. Was God with me here in the wettest American city on the most geographically isolated island chain in the world?

A thunderous clap boomed overhead, yet I recalled how God *remembered* Noah (Genesis 8:1), guided the ark to dry land, and renewed His covenant relationship with him. In the middle of the storm, God gently reminded me of His faithfulness.

Like Noah, I worshipped.

God is with us when we cannot see an end to the darkness. Noah and his family endured over a year of waiting inside the ark before fully glimpsing God's work on the outside. In this world full of trouble (John 16:33), we can expect seasons when we do not understand how God is working. Illness, conflict, and financial hardship can make us assume God has abandoned us.

When we are tempted to misplace our trust, we recall how God used a long period of darkness to protect and preserve Noah's family. Faithfully, He will bring us through our challenging circumstances.

God With Noah

Practice

Think of a time when your situation screamed,
"You are surrounded. There is no escape!"
Did you doubt God's faithfulness?
How does the account of Noah encourage you?

Prayer

Father, help me to trust You in the noise.
Help me see You when I'm alone.
Help me have for You a soft heart to worship.

Promise

Your steadfast love, O Lord, extends to the heavens,
your faithfulness to the clouds.
Psalm 36:5 ESV

~Tracy Harper

God With Us

God with Abraham

DAY 7

*No longer shall your name be called Abram,
but your name shall be Abraham,
for I have made you the father of a multitude of nations.*
Genesis 17:5 NASB

Abram heard his name whispered in the warm wind.

The Lord commanded Abram to leave his home and travel to a new land. God would be with Abram and be his guide. He promised to make Abram a great nation and a blessing to all the families of the earth. Abram took his wife, Sarai, to Canaan, where the childless and aging couple waited with faith.

***

Infertility brings waiting. Our family first grew through adoption. At age thirty-eight, I became drastically ill and miraculously pregnant. God whispered to my heart that I would bear a son. An ultrasound revealed a grapefruit-sized tumor growing with my baby. Waiting for surgery, I prayed not to lose my unborn child. Doubt and fear overtook my faith. I questioned the promise of a son and if God was with me.

Decades of waiting caused Abram to question God's promise. Doubt and fear took over his faith. Abram and Sarai made their plan for a child, but Ishmael was not the son of promise. Yet God was with Abram, even in his faithless act. God renamed Abram—"But your name shall be Abraham, for I have made you the father of a multitude of nations." In his waiting, God transformed Abraham's heart, preparing him to become the Father of many nations with descendants as numerous as the stars. Kings were his legacy.

Keeping faith while waiting for God is hard. Trusting in God's character and His revealed word is required. Faith that depends on circumstances and desired outcomes misses God's heart-transforming work. My son is now twenty-seven years old. Abraham's promised son, Isaac, was the foreshadowing of God's promised Son, Jesus. God is with us.

God With Abraham

Practice

During a time of doubt,
did you contrive to help God,
withdraw from Him, or surrender to His will?

Prayer

Holy Spirit, when waiting makes me doubt,
remind me of Your faithful love.
Help my heart believe Your promises.

Promise

The Scripture, foreseeing that God
would justify the Gentiles by faith,
preached the gospel beforehand to Abraham, saying,
"All the nations will be blessed in you."
Galatians 3:8 NASB

~Claire Alameda

God With Us

PEACE Week Two

*B*elievers experience peace differently than the world. We recognize peace comes to us in the midst of trials. God's unexplainable peace is made known to us in the seasons we need it most.

> *Then you will experience God's peace,*
> *which exceeds anything we can understand.*
> *His peace will guard your hearts and minds*
> *as you live in Christ Jesus.*
> *Philippians 4:7 (NLT)*

As you enter this second week of Advent, may you find peace in the promise that is to come. The narrative leading toward the birth of Jesus continues this week with the lineage of Abraham. His story ushers in the Patriarchs and the time of the Judges. Hard things are ahead, but through it all, God is their source of peace.

~ *Prayer* ~

Lord God, Jehovah,
You are the covenant keeping God.
The promises You give to Your people
bring peace to me today.
May I see them clearly and rest there I
n the challenges of life.
It is in the hard times that I know You are with me
and know Your peace.
Amen

To receive additional resources and discussion questions to guide you through this devotional during Advent, scan the QR code.

God with Isaac

DAY 8

*But Isaac spoke to Abraham his father and said,
"My father!" And he said, "Here I am, my son."
Then he said, "Look, the fire and the wood,
but where is the lamb for a burnt offering?"*
Genesis 22:7 NKJV

Questions raced through Isaac's mind as he climbed Mount Moriah with his father, who assured him God would provide the lamb. When Abraham began binding Isaac, chills ran down the young man's back. As a teenager, Isaac could have overpowered his aged father, but Isaac was obedient. Besides, he couldn't die. God had promised many descendants to him.

Abraham laid Isaac on the wood and raised his knife.

Suddenly, Abraham seemed distracted. Isaac sighed with relief. Something was rustling in the thicket behind them. It was the ram God provided. With joy, father and son offered it to God.

***

Each night incredible pain tormented me. I prayed God would ease the pain, allowing us to sleep. After my spine surgery, nerve damage left me with unwanted complications. Like Isaac desperately searching for the lamb to be sacrificed, I sought relief, but none came quickly. I feared my life would be like this forever.

> *And Abraham called the name of the place,*
> *The-Lord-Will-Provide; as it is said to this day, "*
> *In the Mount of the Lord it shall be provided."*
> Genesis 22:14 NKJV

God was with Isaac when his father was commanded to sacrifice him. Abraham heard the sound of a ram caught up in the thicket, unable to free itself. This became the substitute offering in the place of Isaac.

God was with me when pain and complications eventually subsided, and His mercy prevented things from being worse than they could have been. In His timing He meets our needs. God is Jehovah Jireh, the Lord who provides.

You may have a need in your life God has not met. Don't allow the waiting to shake your faith. God will provide for you as He did for Isaac. God meets the needs of His children in His own timing.

God With Isaac

Practice

What needs are you trusting God
to meet in your life?

Prayer

Father, I know You are my Provider,
but I get inpatient waiting.
I lift these needs to You again today,
and I trust You to do what's best in my life.

Promise

*And my God shall supply all your needs
according to His riches in glory by Christ Jesus.*
Philippians 4:19 NIV

~Carolyn Dale Newell

God With Us

God with Jacob

DAY 9

*Surely the Lord is in this place,
and I was not aware of it.*
Genesis 28:16 NIV

When was the last time you had an encounter with God?

In the ancient land of Canaan lived a man named Jacob. He was the younger twin of Esau, whose birthright Jacob stole. While running for fear of retaliation, Jacob powerfully encountered God in a dream. Even in his running, God was with him.

His story is woven into the tapestry of biblical history through the words of the angel Gabriel to Mary about the baby she would carry. She was told her son would rule over the house of Jacob and its descendants (Luke 1:29–33).

***

There were times when I wondered if God had forgotten about my situation. When I experienced my

God With Us

traumatic brain injury after losing my brother, son, and brother-in-law, I wondered if God knew my pain. He did. He was there. I had just forgotten about his promise to never leave me. The story of Jacob reminds us God is faithful to his promises—and there are so many of them in Scripture!

Jacob's story reminds us there are no perfect people. He was a liar, runner, and cheater. But like God knows you, He knew Jacob. Just as God forgave Jacob, God will forgive you and bless you for His purposes. God knows who you are and has not forgotten you. He has a plan for your life, wants you to seek him, and be obedient to him no matter the circumstance. When we celebrate Christmas, we celebrate not only what took place in Bethlehem. We celebrate God's plan, which started in Eden; flowed through Abraham, Isaac, Jacob, and Jesus; and never ends!

God With Jacob

Practice

Think about encounters you've had with God.
Maybe they were in a dream, through prayer,
or as you were out in nature.
Describe the encounter and how it impacted your life.

Prayer

God, You are always present
and aware of my joys and sorrows.
Help me to trust You more.

Promise

The Lord is good; His mercy endures forever,
and His faithfulness to all generations.
Psalm 100:5 (MEV)

~Janet K Johnson

God With Us

God with Judah

DAY 10

*The scepter will not depart from Judah,
nor the ruler's staff from between his feet,
until he to whom it belongs shall come,
and the obedience of the nations shall be his.*
Genesis 49:10 NIV

Jealousy, hatred, and a murderous plot stained the heart of Judah.

Joseph, the beloved son of Jacob, was detested by Judah and his brothers. Their jealousy for the love of their father corrupted their minds and scarred their hearts. Hatred fueled the flames of destruction their envy could not resist. As these brothers plotted the death of their brother, God intervened. Judah's desire to profit financially influenced the brothers to sell Joseph into slavery and cover their wickedness with a bloody lie. Little did Judah know the plan they devised for evil was part of God's sovereign plan for good and his own survival.

***

There was no murderous plot in my life. Still, the hurt in my heart was profound, and roots of bitterness were burrowing without my recognition. One rejection heaped upon another left me guarded and distant. To protect my heart, I had to protect myself from others. My distance from people did not distance God from me. He was with me, lovingly guiding me on a journey of surrender and hope.

God has a purpose for our lives. While Judah was plotting to kill his brother, God was planning the lineage of the Messiah. Judah was one of many sinful people God used to fulfill His purpose for salvation. Like Judah, we need to recognize our sin, repent, and humble ourselves before the Lord. Our past does not determine our future. God used Judah and his flaws to bring our Messiah. God invites us to surrender ourselves and partner with Him in His beautiful and divine purpose.

Practice

Is your heart hurting?
Have evil thoughts captivated your mind
and taunted your emotions?
Have those emotions led to unholy actions?
God invites you to surrender your hurt to Him
in exchange for hope, healing, and purpose.

Prayer

Father, thank You for inviting me
on a journey of surrender and hope.
I ask You to show me what I need to lay down at the cross
to partner in Your purpose for my life.

Promise

Then one of the elders said to me, "
Do not weep! See, the Lion of the tribe of Judah,
the Root of David, has triumphed.
He is able to open the scroll and its seven seals."
Revelation 5:5 NIV

~Marsha Price

God With Us

God with Tamar

*O*ur expectations may not always be God's.

In Genesis chapter 38, we read that Tamar's heart overflowed with happiness. "Tonight, I shall marry Judah's oldest son and gain respect by having children." Soon her hopes would vanish. Er was wicked in God's eyes, and he died. "Cultural tradition says I must marry Onan, Er's brother. We married, but he also died, refusing to obey his own father by spilling his seed. Devastated, ashamed, and twice widowed, Judah has sent me away to mourn and wait for Shelah to grow older."

***

Culture plays less of a role for women today, yet situations still arise that cause abuse or injustice. Occasionally, relationships or positions produce broken feelings, distrust, or even shame. As a young widow with high hopes for a brighter future, I accepted a job in another state and moved with my twelve-year-old daughter. Three months later all expectations came crashing down around me. Suddenly my world fell apart. I was unjustly fired with no explanation or additional pay. Devastated and emotionally undone, I felt lost, hurt, and ashamed! Where was God?

Did Tamar also have these feelings? She had hopes for children, but Judah had lied about his son. Tamar heard Judah was traveling near her father's house and purposed to sleep with her father-in-law. Would God forgive her?

Adorned in beautiful garments with her face hidden, Tamar waited by the roadside. Judah saw her as a prostitute, and she answered his question shrewdly. "What shall you give me if I sleep with you? We agree. Leave your seal, cord, and staff as a pledge."

Later, Judah discovered Tamar was pregnant. Consequently, he condemned her to death, but she revealed three items she had kept. Shocked, Judah speaks. "She is more righteous than I, since I denied her my son, Shelah."

God was with Tamar! He changed her outcome! She found redemption and access to the lineage of Christ through her twins fathered by Judah.

God with Tamar

Practice

How has your life been redeemed by Jesus
through different situations that appeared hopeless?

Prayer

Thank you, God, for always being there
through every circumstance.
Show me Your way and Your plan
when life's circumstances seem hopeless.

Promise

*There is no wisdom, no insight,
no plan that can succeed against the Lord.*
Proverbs 21:30–31 NIV

~Kathy Watson Swift

God With Us

God with Perez

DAY 11

But then he pulled back his hand, and out came his brother! "What!" the midwife exclaimed. "How did you break out first?" So he was named Perez.
Genesis 38:29 NLT

When was the last time you were surprised?

This was how the midwife and Tamar felt at the birth of Perez. He wasn't expected to be the firstborn. Zerah, Perez's twin brother, had the red cord tied around his wrist when his hand appeared first during birth. But—plot twist—Zerah pulled his hand back in, and then, unexpectedly, Perez made his entrance to the world before his brother.

I can't even imagine being Tamar during this unexpected labor, and I am also a twin mama. Childbirth is scary and painful enough without your babies playing switcheroo. But God was with Perez in this unexpected situation, and Perez carried a reminder of that in his legacy and name, "he who bursts forth."

God is with us in unexpected situations. The unexpected comes in both blessings and challenges. Sometimes they are both, and God is with us in it all. We need only to seek and ask Him to find Him.

***

At the twenty-week ultrasound of my daughter, her heart rate was dangerously high. By the end of the week, we were meeting with a pediatric cardiologist and hearing the diagnosis of fetal supraventricular tachycardia. Our precious daughter had a heart defect. Unexpected, but God was with us. I could feel it.

In the weeks that followed, God was evident at each appointment and in every decision. The doctors had a lifelong plan in place for our daughter with specialists, tests, and medicine, but we had hope and God with us. Though it was the scariest few months of my life, God's presence was palpable.

Then once again the unexpected happened. At her thirty-week ultrasound, a perfectly healthy heartbeat. God is with us in the unexpected, for nothing is unexpected to Him, and we would soon bring into the world our *Selah Hope*.

Practice

Where have you felt God's presence
in an unexpected situation?
How did you know He was there?

Prayer

Father, unexpected things happen,
and You are with me.
Help me to trust and remember that
nothing is unexpected to You.

Promise

*Now all glory to God, who is able,
through his mighty power at work within us,
to accomplish infinitely more than we might ask or think.
Ephesians 3:20 NLT*

~Joy Wendling

God With Us

God with Rahab

*Then Joshua secretly sent out two spies
from the Israelite camp at Acacia Grove.
He instructed them,
"Scout out the land on the other side of the Jordan River,
especially around Jericho."
So the two men set out and came to the house
of a prostitute named Rahab and stayed there that night.*
Joshua 2:1 NLT

What in the world was God doing sending Joshua's men to a prostitute's house?

Joshua received the Lord's orders after the passing of Moses, encouraging him to trust His promise as He led them through the promised land. In preparation to capture the town of Jericho, Joshua would send a few of his men in to spy out the land. As our story begins, a citizen of Jericho tipped off the king that spies had entered the land. Scrambling to find refuge, they knocked on the door of a prostitute and found safety. Rahab seemed to be two steps ahead of them with a plan to hide the men until they could escape.

***

Has God used someone in your life who seemed an unlikely prospect for the situation at hand?

I was a rough-around-the-edges, foul-talking Christian hater who didn't need Jesus as a crutch. Coming from a lifetime of trauma and abuse, my medication of choice was workaholism. I was a six-figure earner success story and one of the few woman senior vice presidents in a male-dominated financial service company.

The other leaders in the company were outspoken Jesus followers who gave Him credit at every opportunity. My eye-roll disdain for these fanatics slowly turned to a journey toward Jesus as He drew me to Himself through some very difficult days.

As God was with Rahab, He was with me.

Even with a checkered past filled with flaws, you are never too far gone. God can use spies or businessmen to draw us into redemption. As Rahab enters a life as one of God's chosen, so I became part of a chosen generation.

Practice

Recall a time when you watched God woo a person
of questionable background,
someone whose life was littered with bad choices,
redeeming and setting them apart for His service.
Maybe that someone was you!
Is anything too hard for God?

Prayer

Father God, thank You for reminding me that
You love to redeem the most unlikely to demonstrate
Your magnificent mercy.
Thank You for helping me not give up on those
who are still resisting You,
knowing you have chosen them. May they choose you.

Promise

*But you are a chosen people, a royal priesthood, a holy nation,
God's special possession, that you may declare the praises
of him who called you out of darkness into his wonderful light.*
Ephesians 2:8–9 NIV

~Athena Dean Holtz

God With Us

God with Salmon

DAY 12

Nahshon was the father of Salmon,
Salmon the father of Boaz.
1 Chronicles 2:11 NIV

Salmon had a role in the ancestry of King David and Jesus and was the father of Boaz.

Although little is said of him in the Scriptures, Salmon was a link in the chain to fulfill the promise. We often search for significance in our roles, but this simple line referencing Salmon reminds us our worth is in our connection to Christ, and our role can seem small but hold great significance in the kingdom. After all, have you heard of Salmon? Often we may feel our roles are small and we won't be remembered, but our connection to Jesus is what matters. People may not have heard of us, but through us will they hear of and know Jesus?

***

Military spouses move, which means we change jobs frequently and are often referenced as the spouse of the military member. This can lead us to ache for identity and long to be seen. Often our roles take on more significance than they should as we search for ways to make an impact. It can be easy to get caught up in our role rather than find our value in Christ.

After a recent move where I left a treasured job, I felt particularly lost. I wondered how God would use me without this position. Salmon's small reference shows that our significance isn't measured by the size of our influence but by our faithfulness to God. We are called to serve God where we are, finding value in every season and role even if it is a simple one like Salmon. Let's be encouraged that as the seasons of life and our roles change, we can cling to God and be steadfast that our impact for the kingdom never wavers and our significance is not found in how big or small our influence but our connection to Jesus.

God With Salmon

Practice

Reflect on a time when you felt your role was insignificant. How does Salmon's story encourage you to see your worth in God's plan, regardless of the size of your influence?

Prayer

Jesus, help us to find our significance in You
and not in our roles and accomplishments.
Remind us that even the smallest acts of faithfulness
can have a great impact in Your kingdom.
Grant us peace and assurance in every season of life,
knowing that our value comes from our connection to You.
Amen.

Promise

*Whatever you do, work at it with all of your heart,
as working for the Lord, not for human masters,
since you know that you will receive
an inheritance from the Lord as a reward.
It is the Lord Christ you are serving.*
Colossians 3:23–24 NIV

~Chantel Mathson

God With Us

God with Boaz

DAY 13

He said, "Who are you?"
And she answered, "I am Ruth, your servant.
Spread your wings over your servant, for you are a redeemer."
Ruth 3:9 ESV

Crossing the field, Boaz suddenly shifted his gaze from his foreman to a woman gleaning in the distance.

Noting her difference, Boaz cocked his ear as his servant connected the stories of the hardworking woman. This was Ruth the Moabite. Impressed? He was more than impressed. Though an outsider, Ruth proved herself compassionate, humble, courageous, and loyal in caring for Naomi, her mother-in-law. Finding Israel's God to be the true God, Ruth trusted Him for her own. The connection made, Boaz covered her with his provision and protection but soon discovered a greater need. As the harvest night neared its end, Ruth's voice trembled as she asked Boaz to be her redeemer.

His mind raced as he thought of her request. Seeking God's guidance, Boaz knew He would be with him in these moments. Already aware of his desire to redeem Ruth, Boaz knew a closer relative had the right. Would this man take the risk, pay the price? Hardly waiting for the day to dawn, Boaz presented the redemption need, but finding the risk too great, Boaz won the honor. Through his selfless act of love, Boaz met Ruth's greatest need as her redeemer. Their story is just a part of a greater redemption story, yours and mine.

***

Our greatest need is a Redeemer. When we are separated from a holy God because of sin, the punishment for sin is death. Because of His great love, God sent His Son, Jesus, who became man and took all sin upon Himself. He paid our penalty through His death on the cross. With acknowledgment of sin and acceptance of God's gracious gift of salvation, each person is redeemed, possessing an eternal hope and inheritance. By securing our redemption, Jesus made a way for us to be with the Father. Just as God was with Boaz in his act of redemption, God is with you as your Redeemer.

God With Boaz

Practice

The Bible is the story of God's redemptive love for you.
What is your redemption story?
Have you been redeemed?

Prayer

Lord, my greatest need was filled
because of Your greatest love.
Thank you for sending Your Son to die in my place,
providing eternal security with You.

Promise

*"But God shows his love for us
in that while we were still sinners,
Christ died for us."*
Romans 5:8 ESV

~Susan Perelka

God With Us

God with Ruth

*Then she knelt face downward, bowing to the ground,
and said to him,
"Why have I found favor in your eyes that you should notice me,
when I am a foreigner?"*
Ruth 2:10 AMP

Ruth gathered grain under the noonday sun as the people nearby sent curious glances her way. She had permission to glean in this field, but as a foreigner, she might have trespassed on some unknown custom. At the other end of the field, the owner came to speak to his servant. Looking up, he saw her. As he approached, Ruth feared she would be sent away with nothing to take home to her mother-in-law. When his instruction to stay and glean from his crops sank in, she fell at his feet. "Why me?" she begged.

He knew of her reputation and honorable acts. "You will be rewarded by the Most High God," he proclaimed.

***

When I moved to Humboldt County, I left behind family and friends. The only person I knew was the man who would one day become my husband and his family. God was with me through the years as I built these relationships and my career. I gained two more daughters and found a body of believers who focused on Him. They brought me in and made me part of their family with Christlike love. My husband and I now grow together in worship and in relationship with our Savior.

When we take upon ourselves His name and fulfill His will for our lives, we see His hand in it. As I look back over the years, the times when I have been obedient to His will for me are the times that I see the fulfillment of His dreams for me. In my husband and family, I can see the miracles He worked to bring this dream to fruition.

Practice

How many times have you moved to a new place
and started over?
Where have you seen God's hand guiding you?

Prayer

Father, we know that You work all things together
for the good of those who love You.
Please help me to know the direction
You want for me and my family.
I know that Your timing isn't always mine,
but it is always perfect.

Promise

So then you are no longer strangers and aliens
[outsiders without rights of citizenship],
but you are fellow citizens with the saints (God's people),
and are [members] of God's household.
Ephesians 2:19 AMP

~Elizabeth Abshire

God With Us

God with Jesse

DAY 14

*Boaz fathered Obed,
Obed fathered Jesse,
and Jesse fathered David.*
Ruth 4:21–22 ESV

I wonder how different our family tree would look if *we* got to choose who's on it.

Here in the book of Ruth, we see Jesse quietly perched on his family tree. God placed him between two Bible heroes: Boaz, his grandfather, a man of strong character, and King David, his son, a man after God's own heart.

***

Like Boaz, I have a grandson named Jesse—the *first boy in seven generations* on my branch of our family tree. Jesse, a sweet, smart, ginger-haired tyke, is now a hardworking young man with a heart for the Lord. His older sister, mom, and grandmas have provided a rich heritage of women going all the way back to his great-great-great-grandmother Stribling. Some of these precious women have left indelible beauty marks on our hearts.

God chooses who comes before and after us. We choose the kind of *legacy* we will leave the generations that follow—whether our family's or others'. In Steve Green's words, "May all who come behind us find us faithful."

A legacy does not just involve material wealth. Timothy's grandmother Lois left him a legacy of *faith* (see 2 Timothy 1:5), which is "of greater worth than gold" (1 Peter 1.7 NIV). Proverbs talks of leaving a legacy of *wisdom* and *righteousness* (Proverbs 8:20, 14:26).

- *Boaz* left a legacy of kindness and integrity to his *grandson* Jesse (Ruth 4).
- *Jesse* left a legacy of hard work to his eight *sons*, including David the future King.
- I will leave *my grandson* Jesse, and my other grandchildren, a legacy. I pray it will be one of faithfulness.

A spiritual legacy is "an enormous value to the next generation … a priceless 'imprint on the future.'" -Brian Dodd.

God With Jesse

Practice

We'll all leave this earth one day.
What kind of imprint on the future do you want to leave
for your family and others?
How can you begin implementing it now?

Prayer

Father, thank You for being with us and with those
You've chosen to come before and after us.
Help us live godly lives that will become
a "heritage of faithfulness" to pass on.

Promise

*Let me proclaim your power to this new generation,
your mighty miracles to all who come after me.*
Psalm 71:18 NLT

~Sandi Banks

God With Us

JOY Week Three

*B*elievers experience joy differently than the world. The world seeks to be happy, but happiness is fleeting. Those of us who know Jesus face life with joy even in suffering.

Dear brothers and sisters, when troubles of any kind come your way,
consider it an opportunity for great joy.
For you know that when your faith is tested,
your endurance has a chance to grow.
James 1:2–3 NLT

As you enter this third week of Advent, may you find joy in the promise that is to come. The narrative leading to the birth of Jesus begins this week with the story of the kings. King David will enter the scene humbly. His life includes great victories and grave trials. Through it all we see the words of his soul penned in the book of the Psalms and find he found great Joy in knowing his God.

~ Prayer ~

Father God, You are a constant source of Joy.
In the trials of life when my faith is tested,
I recognize You are growing me to serve You completely.
May I ever look to You for the source of my joy.
Amen

To receive additional resources and discussion questions to guide you through this devotional during Advent, scan the QR code.

God with David

DAY 15

David continued to succeed in everything he did, for the Lord was with him.
1 Samuel 18:14 NLT

King Saul put David to the test. He raged with jealousy and tried to kill David with his spear, even while David played music to soothe him. Saul was afraid because the Lord had left him and was now with David. Saul made him commander, hoping he would die, but instead David became successful.

It appears David remained submissive to Saul, despite the attempts at his life. Since the Lord was with David, he was protected. He could have simply resisted Saul and ran away, but he didn't.

He remained obedient to his king.

***

God With Us

Slamming the door behind me I blurted, "I give up." It had been one of those days when everything had gone wrong. My anger shot into orbit like a pea from a slingshot, and my lack of patience was put to the test.

So often when my self-limitations are pushed to extinction in my marriage, ministry, or a new venture, I want to quit.

Before I walked out the door that day, I should have realized that all I needed was to ask God for help. Frustration was the result of trying to do it all on my own.

As the Advent season approaches, perhaps you're feeling overwhelmed with decorating, shopping, and planning meals, and anger comes easily. In those times, let us be more like David. Although we may still have spears to dodge, let's look to Jesus for help. If we can capture the realization that the Lord is with us, we already have success within our grasp.

Practice

What challenges do you have in your life
this Christmas season?
Invite God into your life situations to help you
endure these hardships.

Prayer

Father, thank You for the promise
that You are here with me at this very moment.
Please strengthen me to withstand all that I may face today.
Help me to be still in Your presence.
I know it's there that I find all the success I need.
In Jesus's name, amen.

Promise

I know the Lord is always with me.
I will not be shaken, for he is right beside me.
Psalm 16:8 NLT

~Sherri J. Cullison

God With Us

God with Bathsheba

*Then David comforted his wife Bathsheba,
and he went to her and made love to her.
She gave birth to a son, and they named him Solomon.
The LORD loved him; and because the LORD loved him,
He sent word through Nathan the prophet to name him
Jedidiah (Beloved of the LORD).*
2 Samuel 12:24–25 NIV

The dark cloud of grief covers Bathsheba as she once again mourns a loss.

Bathsheba is no stranger to grief. Due to unexpected circumstances, she finds herself in a precarious situation. She is a young, married woman carrying the child of the king; however, he is not her husband. How overwhelming, yet it is just the beginning of her struggles. Shortly after this discovery, her husband, Uriah, is killed, and Scripture tells

God With Us

us "she mourned." In time she married King David and bore his son. Tragedy strikes when the child dies, and once again, the looming cloud of grief consumes Bathsheba. The loss seems too great, but she is comforted by David, and from this union God has a plan. He is with her, and He blesses her with another son, Solomon.

***

Grief is hard, and it comes in many forms—death of a loved one, loss of a relationship, missed opportunities, financial struggles, and unfulfilled expectations.

One day while in the store, the weight of my circumstances became so heavy that breathing and walking were no longer involuntary movements. I had to talk my body through the motions. I looked around, and no one seemed to notice my struggle. I felt so alone in my grief.

I knew I needed to lean into God for His comfort and strength. I prayed, and He graciously placed people in my life to provide for my needs. In these times of weakness, God's power and provision have greater opportunity to be visible and demonstrate how God is with us! Bathsheba experienced significant trauma and grief. Her journey of healing was not linear, yet God was with her, comforted her, and chose her for a divine purpose in the lineage of Christ. Oftentimes we do not see or understand God's plan, but He is always at work, and He is with us!

God with Bathsheba

Practice

When have you felt alone and overwhelmed?
How has God guided you through those difficult times?

Prayer

Almighty God, thank you for continually
being at work around me
and my source of strength through life's ups and downs.
Grant me wisdom and courage as I walk in faith
to pursue Your will for my life.

Promise

*But he said to me, "My grace is sufficient for you,
for my power is made perfect in weakness."
Therefore I will boast all the more gladly about my weaknesses,
so that Christ's power may rest on me.*
2 Corinthians 12:9 NIV

~Bethany Widmer

God With Us

God with Solomon

DAY 16

That night the Lord appeared to Solomon in a dream, and God said, "What do you want? Ask and I will give it to you!"
1 Kings 3:5 NLT

What is one of the best gifts you've ever received? Maybe it was a bike, roller skates, a puppy, a car, or even a child.

King Solomon was a young king who felt overwhelmed, discouraged, and lost. He describes feeling "like a child who doesn't know his way around" (1 Kings 3:7). Solomon prayed and asked God for wisdom. God not only gifted him with wisdom and an understanding heart, but also riches, fame, and a long life (1 Kings 3:10–14).

***

It's easy to feel overwhelmed, discouraged, and alone during all the hustle and bustle of the holidays and preparations. It can be hard to enjoy the small moments.

On December 7, our first foster child arrived at our home. I felt so overwhelmed, anxious, and lost. How would I care for and love this sweet, four-pound baby God (and the state) had entrusted to me? I cried out to God daily asking for wisdom, direction, strength, and peace.

I can only imagine how Mary felt holding baby Jesus for the first time in the coolness and smelliness of the stable. The loud mooing of the cows and the greatest amount of joy and uncertainty. Can you imagine the thoughts going through her mind as not only a first-time mom, but the mother of God's Son? Phew! Talk about feeling overwhelmed!

God was with Solomon, and He is always with us. Just as Solomon asked for the gift of wisdom, we can come to God and ask Him for what we may need. He will always equip us with all we need to fulfill our calling, giving us peace over a situation, strength to care for a loved one, or wisdom on how to raise a teenager or toddler!

God With Solomon

Practice

What is something you are asking God for?

Prayer

Dear God, thank you for being a God I can come to
in times of need.
Please help me in my current situation,
and guide me in the direction I should go.

Promise

If you need wisdom, ask our generous God,
and He will give it to you.
He will not rebuke you for asking.
James 1:5 NLT

~Tracey Druyor

God With Us

God with Rehoboam

DAY 17

But Rehoboam rejected the advice the elders gave him and consulted the young men who had grown up with him and were serving him. The young men replied, "Tell these people who have said to you, 'Your father put a heavy yoke on us, but make our yoke lighter'— tell them, 'My little finger is thicker than my father's waist. My father laid on you a heavy yoke; I will make it even heavier. My father scourged you with whips; I will scourge you with scorpions'"
I Kings 12:10–11 NIV

When God places us in positions to lead or influence others, He is there to help us.

Alone in his chambers, the newly crowned king found himself anxiously pacing. His father, Solomon, had just died, and the future of the kingdom now rested upon his shoulders. Drawn to the table near his bed, Rehoboam picked up the gold scepter. Staring intently at the symbol of his sovereign authority, he pondered the request of the people. In three days they would return to get his answer. Would he grant their desperate petition or, like his father, do what was necessary to secure his own kingdom?

It was by holy design that Israel's kings were to reflect the heart of God to the people. The intent of their Heavenly Father was for the *apple of his eye* to be governed with both justice and mercy. In choosing not to seek God's guidance in response to the people's plea and deciding instead to pursue his own desires, Rehoboam set in motion the prophesied fate of the anguished nation. In disappointment that fueled anger, Israel rebelled, and the kingdom was torn in two; only a remnant remained under the foolish king's rule.

***

We all struggle at times to know what the right thing to do is, but just as He was with Rehoboam, God is with us. Whether it is running a business, parenting children, or doing anything where others look to us for direction, God wants us to recognize He is there to help us. Even when we put our agendas ahead of His and things don't go as we plan, God does not forsake us. He responds to the slightest whisper of His Name. With His wisdom being a treasure beyond compare, He is always faithful to provide the answers we need.

God With Rehoboam

Practice

Rehoboam teaches we fall short of God's plan
and miss his blessings when we
fail to ask for his godly counsel.
Think of a time when you were placed in a position to lead.
How did you respond, and what was the outcome?
What would you do differently today?

Prayer

Father, in the places of my life where You ask me to lead,
I invite Your guidance so I may reflect
Your heart and Your ways.

Promise

I will instruct you and teach you in the way you should go;
I will counsel you with my loving eye upon you.
Psalm 32:8 NIV

~Lori May

God With Us

God with Abijah

DAY 18

God is with us; He is our leader.
With their trumpets, his priests will sound the battle cry against you.
People of Israel, do not fight against the Lord,
the God of your ancestors, for you will not succeed.
2 Chronicles 13:12 KJV

We long to know God is with us when we feel outnumbered or overwhelmed, or need an answer.

The wicked King Abijah reigned in Judah for only three years before he died. "He committed all the sins his father had done before him; his heart was not fully devoted to the Lord his God, as the heart of David his forefather had been" (1 Kings 15:3 NIV). King Abijah attempted to reclaim the northern ten tribes of Israel as part of his kingdom, resulting in a war between Abijah and Jeroboam throughout Abijah's lifetime. Second Chronicles 13 describes a battle in which Abijah triumphed over Jeroboam with his army half the size. King Abijah stood on Mount Zemaraim and spoke out to Northern Israel about God's covenant with David, Abijah announces in today's verse with conviction and sincerity. The troops of Israel had come behind Judah to ambush them. But the men from Judah cried out to God, the priests blew their trumpets, and "at the sound of their battle cry, God routed Jeroboam and all Israel before Abijah and Judah" (2 Chronicles 13:15 NIV). God fought this battle.

***

Moments come in our lives when we must decide to depend on ourselves or God. My husband and I decided to move due to a fantastic job opportunity. We discussed and reasoned but were unsettled and uncertain. We prayed and were given peace and wisdom concerning the answer. We knew we were to make this transition in our life. His answer was immediate, just as He did for Abijah.

The lesson of reliance on God for victory is a recurring theme in the Bible. However, we should never trust a past spiritual accomplishment or season of victory. Our dependence on Him is moment by moment.

Abijah's story encourages and gives us hope. Our dependence on God is the key to our spiritual and earthly victories. We can trust His promises.

Practice

Reflect on a time when Jesus was there for you,
the moment you surrendered to your situation.
Write about the growth you experience
when you rely on Him in your circumstances.

Prayer

Lord, I know You are with me in circumstances
that are more than I can handle.
Please help me understand that You are always there
through every facet of my life
and that I may depend upon You moment by moment.

Promise

I depend on God alone;
I put my hope in Him.
Psalms 62:5 GNT

~Dr. Gayla Campbell

God With Us

God with Asa

DAY 19

*As soon as Asa heard these words, the prophecy ...,
he took courage and put away the detestable idols from all the land
of Judah and Benjamin and from the cities that he had taken
in the hill country of Ephraim,
and he repaired the altar of the LORD that was in the front
of the vestibule of the house of the LORD.*
2 Chronicles 15:8 ESV

Fiery indignation burned in King Asa's heart as he saw the horrific idols that littered the land of Judah and Benjamin. Inspired by the words of the prophet Azariah to be strong in the Lord and not forsake Him, Asa took courage (2 Chronicles 15:8) and got rid of all the abominable images from the land, including one very important one—the detestable image of Asherah constructed at the order of Asa's grandmother, Maacah, the queen mother. Asa demolished this image too and had his grandmother deposed of her title as queen mother (2 Chronicles 15:16).

***

For many of us, acceptance by our family is our idol, and there is nothing we won't do to avoid their rejection. As a child, I often walked on eggshells to please my mom regardless of what she asked of me. Very sensitive to her critical nature, I feared her negative reactions the most. When I became the only Christian in my family, I had a tough decision to make: to fear God or man. I wanted to obey God and share the gospel, but I was afraid my mom wouldn't understand or accept my newfound faith. Nevertheless, God was with me and emboldened me to share my testimony of new life in Him. Despite my mom's harsh and ignorant response, I took many opportunities to share my faith with her until her dying breath.

All believers have moments in their lives when the rubber meets the road. Will we obey the Lord or choose the approval of man over God? Asa heard the prophet's words. We need to be in God's word rehearsing His commands and promises. Prayer support cannot be overestimated. Over the years, I had many prayer warriors storming heaven's gates on my behalf when I spent time with my mother.

God With Asa

Practice

Think of a time when you had to bolster your courage
to obey God over pleasing a loved one.
How did reading God's Word
and enlisting prayer support help you?
How did God show He was with you?

Prayer

Lord, please give us determination and strength
to fear You more than man,
especially when we may disappoint a loved one.

Promise

The Lord is my helper;
I will not fear; what can man do to me?
Hebrews 13:6 ESV

~Page Gyatt

God With Us

God with Jehoshaphat

DAY 20

You will not have to fight this battle. Take up your positions; stand firm and see the deliverance the LORD will give you, Judah and Jerusalem. Do not be afraid; do not be discouraged. Go out to face them tomorrow, and the LORD will be with you.
2 Chronicles 20:17 NIV

"A vast army is coming against you." The warning came of two armies approaching to attack Judah. "Alarmed, Jehoshaphat, resolved to inquire of the Lord, and he proclaimed a fast for all Judah. The people of Judah came together to seek help from the Lord." Jehoshaphat prayed, "If calamity comes upon us, … we will stand in Your presence … and cry out to you … we do not know what to do, but our eyes are on you" (2 Chronicles 20:2–4, 9, 12 NIV).

The Spirit spoke to them through Jahaziel, the priest. "Do not be afraid or discouraged … the battle is not yours, but God's … go out and face them … the Lord will be with you" (2 Chronicles 20:15, 17 NIV).

Preparing to set out, Jehoshaphat told them, "Have faith in the Lord your God and you will be upheld … you will be successful" (2 Chronicles 20:20 NIV).

They sent the worship team ahead of the army, singing praises to God. As they began to sing, God set ambushes. When they arrived at the scene, there were only dead bodies. The armies had destroyed one another. Victory was theirs without a battle.

***

My husband died unexpectedly. My world was turned upside down. Many decisions swirled around me, and I didn't know what to do. I called out to God, and many people prayed for us. Even when my reeling brain struggled to string words together, prayers for specific needs brought unexpected provisions at timely moments.

God is with us when we are facing trouble. We can follow Jehoshaphat's example when troubles come our way. When we don't know what to do, we can resolve to inquire of the Lord and seek His help because He is with us. We can stand in His presence with our eyes on Him knowing He will watch over us and accomplish His purposes.

God With Jehoshaphat

Practice

How will you inquire of the Lord
about a current struggle?

Prayer

Lord, I do not know what to do.
You are with me in this struggle.
Give me the wisdom I need.
Strengthen me to persevere and stand firm.

Promise

*You are my hiding place; you will protect me
from trouble and surround me with songs of deliverance.*
Psalm 32:7 NIV

~Liz Holtzman

God With Us

God with Uzziah

DAY 21

*Whatever you do, work at it with all your heart,
as working for the Lord, not for human masters,
since you know that you will receive an inheritance from the Lord
as a reward. It is the Lord Christ you are serving.*
Colossians 3:23–24 NIV

"Never get too big for your britches, little girl!" If I heard that once, I heard it hundreds of times. Being the indulged only child, I fancied myself capable of doing anything and everything. After all, I thought I was the center of the universe. But the harsh reality hit when my flaws became apparent to me and everyone else. I had stood on the pedestal of my pride, and it crumbled beneath me. This seems to be the story of King Uzziah too.

King Uzziah was known for his many military and architectural achievements during his fifty-two-year reign over Judah in the eighth century BC, yet he failed to lead his people spiritually. Second Chronicles 26:4–5 highlights that King Uzziah prospered as long as he obeyed God's commands—God was with Uzziah. His downfall was recorded in 2 Chronicles 26:16 when he overstepped his role. In his attempt to perform the duties assigned only to priests, he violated God's divine order. Pride led to his downfall, and he spent his later years suffering from leprosy.

Had King Uzziah recognized he was supposed to work for God's glory and not his own, his pride might have been tempered, and he might not have "gotten too big for his britches." We must live by faith knowing God is pleased when we serve Him. He is at work in all our efforts, whether we see results or not, and He is using us to further His purposes, not ours.

Practice

Pause and reflect on a time when God
might not have been your priority.
If He is not receiving the credit,
perhaps it's time to ponder whom you truly hold
in the highest esteem.

Prayer

Father, humble my heart.
May I always fix my gaze on You,
seeking only to do Your will.

Promise

Therefore, my dear brothers and sisters, stand firm.
Let nothing move you.
Always give yourselves fully to the work of the Lord,
because you know that your labor in the Lord is not in vain.
2 Corinthians 15:58 NIV

~Jackie Freeman

God With Us

LOVE Week Four

Believers experience love differently than the world. The world seeks to be satisfied with a love that comes from others, but we are satisfied because of the love that comes from God.

> *See how very much our Father loves us,*
> *for he calls us his children, and that is what we are!*
> *But the people who belong to this world don't recognize*
> *that we are God's children because they don't know him.*
> *James 1:2–3 NLT*

As you enter this fourth week of Advent, may you find love in the promise that is to come. The narrative introduces us to Joseph, the earthly father of Jesus. How great was Joseph's love for Mary as he walked a hard road of obedience to bring the Savior into the world. His love displayed allows us to see the love of our Heavenly Father adopting us to become His children and heirs of the kingdom.

~ Prayer ~

Father God, You demonstrate Your love to me
on the pages of Scripture.
All you offer in the storyline of Jesus reveals this to me.
Thank you for loving me and using people just like me
to bring Jesus into this world.
May my love for you be demonstrated
in a life that seeks You alone.
Amen

To receive additional resources and discussion questions to guide you through this devotional during Advent, scan the QR code.

God with Ahaz

DAY 22

For the LORD humbled Judah because of King Ahaz of Judah,
who threw off restraint in Judah
and was unfaithful to the LORD.
2 Chronicles 28:19 CSB

Could God possibly be with a corrupt leader whose moral compass is oriented only toward himself?

God humbled the entire nation of Judah because of wicked king Ahaz. For Ahaz, "throwing off restraint" included burning his sons as offerings to pagan gods and stripping gold from God's temple to pay an Assyrian king to protect Judah from military attack. That payoff did not pay off, and Judah suffered horrendous losses. Later, Ahaz made sacrifices at a pagan altar he installed inside the Lord's temple before eventually shutting its doors completely.

Yet Ahaz is listed in the genealogy of Christ. God clearly had a plan.

God allowed the natural consequences of Ahaz's wicked leadership to unfold, affecting the entire nation. But He did not abandon Judah, nor did he cut off Ahaz's family. Despite the depravity of Ahaz, God preserved one of his sons. When Hezekiah became king, he immediately set out to right the wrongs of his father.

"If we are unfaithful, he remains faithful, for he cannot deny who he is" (2 Timothy 2:13 NLT). God's character doesn't change. He is gracious to us because of His nature, not because of ours. He extends His love even in the face of the worst behavior.

We know what it is to live in a culture that has thrown off restraint. Headlines shout stories of brokenness that must surely break the heart of God. Our world may be filled with chaos and corruption, but God is still on the throne. He is with us, because His love never changes.

God With Ahaz

Practice

What does God's faithfulness despite Ahaz's unfaithfulness
show you about His character?
How does God's faithfulness encourage you as you live
in a culture that has "thrown off restraint"?

Prayer

God help me to trust that You are with me in a broken
world even when all appearances are to the contrary.
Remind me of Your faithfulness in the face of faithlessness,
whether my own or those around me.
Increase my understanding of Your grace.

Promise

*"Though the mountains be shaken and the hills be removed,
yet my unfailing love for you will not be shaken n
or my covenant of peace be removed,"
says the* LORD, *who has compassion on you.*
Isaiah 54:10 NIV

~Elizabeth Renicks

God With Us

God with Hezekiah

DAY 23

*Be strong and courageous; do not be afraid nor dismayed
before the king of Assyria,
nor before all the multitude that is with him;
for there are more with us than with him.
With him is an arm of flesh; but with us is the Lord our God,
to help us and to fight our battles.*
2 Chronicles 32:7–8 NKJV

Second only to King David, Hezekiah would become known as the greatest king in the history of God's people.

There would be no "like father like son" in Hezekiah's story. His father, King Ahaz, did what was wrong in the Lord's sight, provoking the anger of God, plundering, and shutting the doors of the house of the Lord. Unlike his father, Hezekiah did what was right in the Lord's sight. He immediately opened and repaired the doors of the house of

God With Us

the Lord, ushering in worship and consecrating a nation to serve the one true and living God.

Hezekiah's life would be marked by two particularly insurmountable battles: threats of a fierce clash with the mighty Assyrian empire and a personal struggle against an illness that threatened to claim his life. Two vastly different battles, yet one common thread.

Hezekiah prayed. God heard. God answered.

The first battle found the evil king of Assyria sending messengers to taunt the people of Jerusalem and deliver a warning letter to Hezekiah to surrender—or else! After reading the letter, Hezekiah went up to the house of the Lord, spread out the letter before the Lord, and prayed (2 Kings 19:14–15).

Picture Hezekiah taking that letter and laying it out before the Lord. If you read his prayer in verses 15–19, you'll observe a man acknowledging who God is and then pouring out his need to the only one He knew who could save and deliver them.

God With Hezekiah

Practice

What is your insurmountable need?
Pour out your heart to the Lord.
He is able and trustworthy.
You can count on Him to hear your prayers
and hold you until the answer comes.

Prayer

Father, I confess that I cannot fight these battles alone.
I desperately need You.
Help me to trust You with my insurmountable needs.

Promise

"Be anxious for nothing,
but in everything by prayer and supplication,
with thanksgiving,
let your requests be made known to God.
Philippians 4:6 NKJV

~Shelly Brown

God With Us

God with Josiah

DAY 24

When the King heard what was written in the Book of the Law, he tore his clothes in despair.
2 Kings 22:11 NLT

God uses history for His good.

God removed the evil influences in Josiah's life during his formative years, allowing him to seek the God of David with all his heart, soul, and might. He had wise godly counsel around him, but it wasn't until he heard the Word of God read aloud that he realized all was doomed because the nation had turned from God.

Hearing the law grieved him and made him seek God even more. Josiah fulfilled a three-hundred-year-old prophecy by removing all the idols from the land and allowed his people to worship the one true God freely.

He honored God by introducing the celebration of Passover, a feast not celebrated since the time of Samuel.

God With Us

Because Josiah sought the Lord, God delayed the punishment for thirty-one years.

***

At the age of eleven, I watched a movie that made me question the validity of the Scripture used in a court scene —or was it just Hollywood adding to the horrific storyline in the movie?

Alone in my bedroom, I looked up the verses in Revelation in question. The movie was *Helter Skelter*, and the Scripture discussed was about the seal of the Lord on His children's forehead.

As I read the Scripture, I realized I would face the punishment the unsaved would face. At that moment, I knew my heart was not filled with godly things, no Scriptures were in my heart even though I went to church regularly.

A decision that night would change my life and give me a Rescuer and Rock to lean on all my days. God was with me that night as I processed the disturbing movie scenes and the reality of a life without Him in it.

Practice

Think of a time the truth of Scripture
grieved your sinful soul.
How did you respond to your grief?

Prayer

Abba Father, thank You for Your written Word.
What a glorious godly example Josiah was
because he sought You with all His heart, soul, and might.
Help us to follow that example in all we do.

Promise

Seek the Kingdom of God and His above all else
and live righteously,
and He will give you everything you need.
Matthew 6:33 NLT

~Crystal Manget

God With Us

God with Jechoniah

DAY 25

*"Thus says the Lord, the God of Israel: '
Like these good figs, so I will acknowledge
those who are carried away captive from Judah,
whom I have sent out of this place for their own good,
into the land of the Chaldeans.'"*
Jeremiah 24:5 NKJV

As the Babylonian army marched toward the city to besiege it, the Israelites continued to stray further from the Lord and His commands. Unaware of the impending judgment, they disobeyed His law and let their hearts grow cold in their love for Him.

King Jeconiah took the throne of Israel at eighteen years old. His father, King Jehoiakim, did evil in the sight of the Lord; King Jeconiah followed in his father's footsteps. The days were dark for the people of Israel as the world they knew was destroyed. They wondered if God would keep His promises and save them. Held captive in Babylon, they wondered how the promised Messiah would come if Israel was destroyed.

King Jeconiah did not lead well and found himself in prison for thirty-seven years. When released, he was brought into King Evil-Merodach's presence. He spoke kindly to Jeconiah and invited him to eat at his table all the days of his life. His life was not only preserved, but he was under the king's care. The Lord watched over Jeconiah even in his disobedience and preserved His promise. He was working His plans for good even when it looked dark. Indeed, God was with him.

***

My husband and I were in a season of darkness when the plans of the Lord felt impossible. I questioned if God was with me. We lost our baby, the sister our daughter had fervently prayed for and the one who would complete our family. Everything seemed wrong, dark, and without hope, but God continued to write our story and brought His perfect plans to fruition. A baby girl joined our family through adoption just eight months later. A God-sized story amid the brokenness of our hearts and the darkness of this world.

God With Jechoniah

Practice

When have you walked through darkness?
When you look back, can you see God was with you,
preserving your story and His plan?

Prayer

Father, help me to trust You when the darkness comes.
Give me faith to remember You are with me
and courage to walk in boldness knowing
You are working all things for Your good plan.

Promise

*And we know that all things work together for good
to those who love God,
to those who are called according to his purpose.
Romans. 8:28 NKJV*

~Janell Neumann

God With Us

God with Zerubbabel

DAY 26

*This is the word of the LORD to Zerubbabel:
"Not by might nor by power, but by my Spirit,"
says the LORD Almighty.*
Zechariah 4:6 NIV

Everything came to a screeching halt when they chose fear over faith!

Zerubbabel was commissioned as governor under King Cyrus of Persia to lead the first wave of liberated exiles from Babylon to their homeland in Jerusalem to rebuild the temple. As the work began, so did the opposition. It came quickly! Rather than trust God and oppose the opposition, fear and discouragement reigned, and work on the temple stopped for sixteen years! God promised Zerubbabel would lay the foundation of the temple and that his hands would also complete it—and God is a promise keeper!

***

God With Us

We sometimes question God's assignment in our lives when things don't go as planned and we give up or quit. After my husband of thirty-five years went to be with the Lord, I questioned God's call to continue the ministry as a new widow. I didn't want or know how to lead a ministry. God reminded me that it wasn't my ministry; it was His. He promised if I trusted Him, He would guide me—by His Spirit, not by my skill or ability.

It's been fifteen years, and God has been faithful to His promise! God promised He would be with Zerubbabel and told him not to fear. He sent the prophets Haggai and Zechariah to Zerubbabel to call them back to finish the task of building the temple. Just like Zerubbabel, God has brought people into my life to encourage me to finish my assignment!

God With Zerubbabel

Practice

What unfinished assignment
have you've been ignoring or fearful to tackle?
How does Zerubbabel's going back after sixteen long years
to finish building the temple encourage you
to step out now and with God's help
complete the assignment He has given you
regardless of how long it's been?

Prayer

Lord, remind me of my utter inability
to accomplish anything apart from You
but that with You nothing is impossible!
Give me the strength by your Spirit to finish
the assignment You have given me.

Promise

Trust in the LORD with all your heart
and lean not on your own understanding;
in all your ways submit to him,
and he will make your paths straight.
Proverbs 3:5–6 NIV

~Sara Beekman

God With Us

God with Joseph

DAY 27

*An angel of the Lord appeared to him in a dream and said,
"Joseph son of David, do not be afraid
to take Mary home as your wife,
because what is conceived in her is from the Holy Spirit."*
Matthew 1:20 NIV

Deep satisfaction tingled through Joseph's fingers. The wood's imperfections yielded to his touch. Beeswax would seal the table's beauty, providing a durable surface for family meals.

Family. The word pierced his heart deeper than the roots of the tallest cedar. Mary—his betrothed, pregnant with another man's child.

What is worse? Joseph wondered. *That she betrayed me or God? Should I expose her? Should I marry her? What about my reputation? People will assume I committed this unthinkable sin. I thought she was the one. If I divorce her quietly, it might protect her from public shame. It's the right thing to do.*

God With Us

"Lord," Joseph prayed, "I don't understand. You have always been faithful. When the perfect cedar for my project fell at the ax of another carpenter, You provided a more perfect one in the forest beyond. I trust You now to provide a more perfect wife. Adonai."

Instead, God provided a dream. "Do not be afraid to take Mary home as your wife," the angel said. Joseph was at a crossroads. The logical choice was divorce. The courageous choice was to trust God instead of relying on his own understanding. Imagine God's trust in Joseph to choose him to be the stepfather of His Son! God trusted Joseph. Joseph trusted God.

***

Our crossroads were found spread out on the conference table. Within the stacks of paper, the undisclosed hiccup awaited our signature. Another setback in our frustrating house-hunting saga. Throughout our search God faithfully revealed flaws, then provided a better option. This hiccup didn't surprise God. Did He trust us to trust Him? God proved His faithfulness and we trusted Him.

Life has many crossroads. Logically, trust requires knowledge of the facts. Whereas faith requires trust in God regardless of our own understanding. Do you trust God as much as He trusts you?

Practice

What crossroad is God trusting you to trust Him?
How will God's faithfulness in the past
enable you to trust Him with your future?
Consider God's faith and trust in you.

Prayer

Lord Jesus, when I stand at the crossroads,
fill me with courage to trust You
instead of relying on my own understanding.
It is Your faithfulness that enables me to faithfully trust
You regardless of the circumstances.

Promise

Trust in the Lord with all your heart,
And lean not on your own understanding;
In all your ways acknowledge Him,
And He shall direct your paths.
Proverbs 3:5–6 NKJV

~Marie T. Palecek

God With Us

God with Mary

> *But the angel said to her,*
> *"Do not be afraid, Mary; you have found favor with God.*
> *You will conceive and give birth to a son,*
> *and you are to call him Jesus."*
> Luke 1:30–31 NIV

"Impossible! What will my parents <u>think?</u>

"I'm not even married yet. How could I be pregnant and have favor with God?"

Mary left the city to go to an oasis in the hill country to visit Zechariah the priest and her cousin Elizabeth. She needed solitude and peace. Each step uphill grew her inner strength. Once her eyes landed on Elizabeth's poochy stomach with her first child, the angel's words came to life, and she began singing. Her courage to carry God incarnate inserted Mary into God's story line.

God With Us

***

My mother's name was Mary, and she, too, carried the fear of revealing her secret pregnancy. But when my daddy passed suddenly, my mom felt it was safe to reveal the hidden family secret. Tears streamed down her face, and her voice trembled as she waited on judgment. Both raised in church, Mom shared about their surprise pregnancy with my sister.

Did an angel visit Mom? Did God use Mom's sister and husband to encourage her? Like Mary and Elizabeth being pregnant with their first child at the same time, Mom journeyed to motherhood at the same time with her sister.

Quickly, our parents had a shotgun wedding and then divorced too soon. Then a second pregnancy surprised them. Me!

Church bells rang this time as a gift to their mothers two days before Christmas. God gave us the gift of family for forty years, separated only by Dad's death. Instead of judgment, God gave Mom favor with her two girls. Our respect blossomed for her choosing the gift of life not once, but twice.

When faced with impossibilities, have you ever felt judged? Mary retreated to an oasis to seek godly counsel. During her time with Elizabeth, God blessed her with peace and encouragement.

Mary blessed us with the gift of Jesus Christ, Immanuel, God with us.

God with Mary

Practice

Pregnancies out of the ordinary were used
to carry God's miracles.
God carried Mary the mother of Jesus and my mother,
Mary, until they had strength to walk uphill on their own.
Courage brought peace, and judgment turned into a gift.
How has God done the same for you?

Prayer

Mighty Father, when I'm faced with
impossible circumstances, help me not fear judgment.
Lift my eyes as You carry me in the midst of the storm.
Please bless me with courage to
walk on my own toward Your divine plan.

Promise

*When Elizabeth heard Mary's greeting, the baby leaped in her womb,
and Elizabeth was filled with the Holy Spirit.
In a loud voice she exclaimed: "Blessed are you among women,
and blessed is the child you will bear!"*
Luke 1:41–42 NIV

~Leasha Rutschman

God With Us

God with Mary

Practice

Pregnancies out of the ordinary were used
to carry God's miracles.
God carried Mary the mother of Jesus and my mother,
Mary, until they had strength to walk uphill on their own.
Courage brought peace, and judgment turned into a gift.
How has God done the same for you?

Prayer

Mighty Father, when I'm faced with
impossible circumstances, help me not fear judgment.
Lift my eyes as You carry me in the midst of the storm.
Please bless me with courage to
walk on my own toward Your divine plan.

Promise

*When Elizabeth heard Mary's greeting, the baby leaped in her womb,
and Elizabeth was filled with the Holy Spirit.
In a loud voice she exclaimed: "Blessed are you among women,
and blessed is the child you will bear!"*
Luke 1:41–42 NIV

~Leasha Rutschman

God With Us

JESUS
hope • peace • joy • love

Believers experience Christmas differently because of Jesus. This is more than just a day to celebrate with food, family, and gifts under the tree. This is a day when we celebrate the birth of the One who will rescue us from ourselves because of His great love.

As we leave the holiday season behind us for another year, may you find a place for Jesus in your life. Advent brings a beautiful reminder of hope, peace, joy, and love, but they are not just for the season. Walk in the life Jesus offers and rest in His hope, peace, joy, and love all year long. Continue to grow in knowing Him through reading His Word, fellowshipping with believers, and communicating in prayer.

*Therefore, go and make disciples of all the nations,
baptizing them in the name of the Father
and the Son and the Holy Spirit.
Teach these new disciples to obey all the commands I have given you.
And be sure of this: I am with you always, even to the end of the age.
Matthew 28:19–20 NLT*

You are part of God's family and bring His story into the world by sharing the gospel with others. Bring the hope, peace, joy, and love you have found in Jesus to everyone you know. This is the call on your life and there you will find He is with you!

~ *Prayer* ~

Dear Jesus,
Thank You for entering our world as a baby, so humble.
Thank You for living a perfect life
and being the sacrifice for my sin.
You have brought me hope, peace, joy, and love.
May I share this with my world
so they will come to know You.
Amen

Immanuel, God with Us

DAY 28

So the Word became human and made his home among us.
He was full of unfailing love and faithfulness.
And we have seen his glory,
the glory of the Father's one and only Son.
John 1:14 NLT

Heaven's birthday celebration erupted with Jesus's earthly arrival! Angels' amplifying horns reverberated, and confetti of shooting stars worshipped across the night sky. Singing at the top of their lungs, the angelic choir declared:

"Glory to God in highest heaven,
and peace on earth to those with whom God is pleased!"
Luke 2:14 NLT

Jesus's delivery was in the most unprivileged and disgusting place. Such a glorious event began in horrible surroundings. Baby Jesus was wrapped in swaddling clothes and placed on top of dirty, smelly yuck. And still, all of heaven proclaimed God's grandeur with His entrance. Jesus deserved better, but God had a plan and a purpose to be with us. So He sent His precious one and only Son to save sinners.

The foul barn stable represents the dirtiest part of ourselves, and Jesus, in His holiness, was laid among what defiles us—our sins. His truths enlighten our disobedience, revealing where we fall short of God's glory. Yet He is always with us amid our messiness.

Focusing on His love, mercy, and forgiveness will lead our hearts to confess our sins. And God gives us purification as we cooperatively relinquish them. Through our cleansing, His faithfulness offers us an abundance of grace and peace. The beauty of our deliverance from our sinful lives is to be clothed in His righteousness as God's Spirit desires.

Excitedly, yet humbly, welcome Jesus so you, too, can receive new birth into a God-designed life with exclusive devotion. May your soul bellow in heavenly songs of praise to Immanuel, God with us!

Immanuel, God With Us

Practice

Is there a sin you need to bring before Jesus
to allow His transformation in you?
What can you bring to Immanuel,
packaged with a beautiful bow of humility
to display your love for Him?

Prayer

Abba Daddy, I praise You for who You are
and for always being with me,
no matter my circumstances.
Cleanse me in the areas I willingly surrender to You.
Forgive me, and bring me into Your loving embrace.
I long to know You more intimately.

Promise

For the LORD your God is living among you.
He is a mighty savior. He will take delight in you with gladness.
With his love, he will calm all your fears.
He will rejoice over you with joyful songs.
Zephaniah 3:17 NLT

~Maureen Wild

God With Us

Contributing Authors

Elizabeth Abshire is an author and retired public safety dispatcher who lives in the coastal redwoods of California, where she loves to hunt and fish with her husband, Martin, and play with her grandchildren. Author of *To the Moon and Back* and *Finding the Blessings*. (blessedandrestored.com)

Claire Alameda is a missionary, Bible teacher, speaker, and cross-cultural trainer. She cofounded Corazón Ministries, where she directs women's programs. Her most treasured role is mentoring young women to connect culturally with the Gospel and grow in their faith. (clairealameda@gmail.com)

Sandi Banks is a published author and devotional writer for numerous publishing houses. As a storyteller, Sandi draws inspiration from her adventures and misadventures through forty countries on six continents. She has served thirty years on the Speak Up staff. (sandibanks.com)

Sara Beekman has a contagious passion to tell others about Jesus and inspire women to grow deeper in their walk with God. She continues to give leadership to the nonprofit ministry that she and her husband founded together in 1989. (stoptopray.org)

Faith Blum is a wife, mom, author, and pianist. She writes Christian historical adventure fiction featuring faith-strengthening romance. When not writing, she can be found cooking from scratch, reading, spending time with her husband, or chasing her high-energy son.

Shelly Brown coleads hybrid publishing company Redemption Press. She serves with Love UnVeiled, a transformational discipleship ministry that helps women experience healing, transformation, and freedom. She resides in Orlando, Florida, where her favorite role is GaGa to three beautiful grandgirls.
(shellyb@redemption-press.com)

Dr. Campbell is an award-winning author of *Pursuing God's Heart: A Bible Study of Jonah*. She is also a speaker, BMI songwriter, musician, and counselor. Texas is where she enjoys family life, serving her community, and church. Gayla and her husband are co-executives of G&G Ministries. (gandgministries.org)

Sherri Cullison shares her powerful God-story to encourage others as an author, speaker, and survivor. With one husband, two kids, seven grandkids, five pianos, and one RZR, she loves leading worship, traveling, and RZR rides. (sherrijcullison.com)

Tracey Druyor was born in Illinois and is currently a pastor's wife in Arizona. A mom of five children, she is passionate about foster care, adoption, special needs, and mental health. Some of her favorite things are dogs, music, and reading. (tdruyor@gmail.com)

Cherie Fletcher is the author of *God's Precious Jewels* and *The Believer's Walk*. She is an evangelist, a lay chaplain for the Henry County Sheriff's Department, a member of her church's Health and Wellness Committee, and a registered nurse. She lives in Georgia with her husband and loves car trips, sightseeing, and cooking. (ckfletcher6@gmail.com)

Jackie Freeman is an author and speaker who has enchanted readers with her delightful children's picture books, heartfelt devotionals, and journals. You will be charmed by her wit and wisdom, as many of her stories revolve around her family's farm in southeast Michigan. (jackiefreemanauthor.com)

Page Gyatt is a retired ESL teacher, Bible-study teacher, author, mother, and grandmother. She lives in Virginia, where she enjoys reading, writing, studying the Bible, working out, and playing pickleball.
(pglovejoyhope@gmail.com)

Tracy Harper is an author, speaker, and missionary. She writes devotions that reset your relationship with God. Her book on avoiding counterfeit guidance by facilitating a relationship with the Holy Spirit will be released in 2025. (tracyharperwrites.com)

Athena Dean Holtz is an author, speaker, podcaster, and publisher at Redemption Press. She and her pastor-turned-writing-coach hubby live in a quaint little town in the foothills of Mount Rainier. She and Ross coauthored *Together for a Purpose: Love and Mission in Marriage and Ministry.* (athenadeanholtz.com)

Liz Holtzman is an intercessor, a speaker, and the author of *Proven Character: Praying for Our Children*. She is passionate about teaching people to be intentional and strategic in prayer. She believes prayer creates spiritual space for God's work. (lizholtzman.com)

Janet K Johnson is an award-winning author, speaker, spiritual mentor, wife, mother, and grandmother. Her heart's passion is to help people heal well from life's tragedies as they experience God's presence and joy amid their losses. (janetkjohnson.com)

Jerri Lien is an author with Redemption Press. She has published two children's picture books, *Bixby and the Very Bad Idea* and *Bixby and the Very Jolly Christmas.* Jerri has also published devotions in conjunction with Redemption Press devotional compilations. She lives in Arizona with her husband, Scott, and dog, Bixby. (jerrilien.com)

Angela Mackey is a nurse, author, and speaker as well as a wife and mom. She encourages people to reconsider their thinking in light of God's word that they may live transformed. Angela loves coffee, Kansas basketball, and reading books. (rethinkingmythinking.com)

Crystal Manget is a Christian wife, mother, writer, artist, personal chef, and blogger. She loves crafts and travel. (graceadditives.com)

Chantel Mathson: CEO of Inspirational Inc. and founder of "Tea With Chantel" trainings. A keynote speaker, blogger, Bible teacher, author, host, and business professor. As a military spouse and mom, she loves connecting over tea, inspiring others one cup at a time. (teawithchantel.com)

Lori May, with degrees in biblical studies and clinical mental health, served in full-time ministry and built a thriving counseling practice. Lori shares a home on the beautiful Oregon coast with her husband of twenty years and her father. (facebook.com/lori.w.may)

Janell Neumann is the director of children's ministry at her church and a homeschooling mom of four. She and her husband, Jason, reside in Mesa, Arizona. She enjoys time with her family and helping other midlife mamas navigate the "messy middle" through mentoring and speaking. (janellneumann@gmail.com)

Carolyn Dale Newell is a speaker and the author of six books. She lives with blindness but calls it a gift from God. She lives in Virginia with her husband, Tim, and adorable guide dog, Iva. (amountainoffaith.com)

Marie T. Palecek is a passionate author and speaker. Her transformational devotional, *Listen for His Voice*, Bible-study journals, and speaking engagements inspire audiences to listen for God's voice amid life's challenges and the mundane. She enjoys life in beautiful Minnesota. (marietpalecek.com)

Susan Perelka lives with her husband and four children in Northeast Ohio surrounded by the beautiful Cuyahoga Valley National Park, where she often enjoys walking. Her debut release is *Trust in Every Moment: A Journey toward God*. (susannperelka.com)

Elizabeth Renicks is an author, speaker, and teacher. She uses truth and tools from the Bible to help women cultivate intimate relationship with God. A wife and boy mom, Elizabeth calls Tuscaloosa, Alabama, home. (elizabethrenicks.com)

Leasha Rutschman is a Christian author and works in financial services. She and her husband live in Wichita, Kansas, and love cooking for family and friends in their home. Leasha has a heart for encouraging ladies grieving and caregiving. (Facebook and Instagram)

Marsha Price is a follower of Jesus Christ, wife, mother, and ministry leader. She lives in Arizona with her husband near their two adult children. She has served in women's ministry over two decades. Her passion is helping women understand their identity in Christ and their purpose in life. (marsha-price.com)

Kathy Watson Swift is a career missionary, motivational speaker, and author. She passionately loves God, her husband, her children, her grandchildren, and countless others across three continents. Kathy's life adventures will turn your thoughts upward, knowing that God's love never fails! (freedomhmin.org)

Carol Tetzlaff is an author, speaker, and associate publisher for Redemption Press. She loves all things yellow, supersweet iced coffee, and living in Arizona with her husband and their family. Author of *Ezra: Unleashing the Power of Praise: A 7-Week Bible Study*. (caroltetzlaff.com)

Joy Wendling is a family pastor, parent coach, and speaker. She encourages mamas to use purposeful play to discipline and disciple their children on her podcast, *Playfully Faithful Parenting*. (createdtoplay.com)

Bethany Widmer is an author, speaker, and certified life coach. Her passion is encouraging others to pursue their God-given calling. She and her husband, Scott, lead marriage ministry and enjoy spending time with their daughters, Samantha, Emma, and Sophia. (sincerelybethany.com)

Maureen Wild is an author, speaker, and wellness advocate. She is married to Mike and is dog mom to Daisy, her beloved rescue. Maureen wants all to be WILD in Jesus and obtain root-cause healing—physically, emotionally, and spiritually. (wildinjesus.com)

This devotional is a compilation of writings
from authors from the
Redemption Press Devotional Challenge 2023.
To order please go to redemption-press.com
or wherever books are sold.

REDEMPTION PRESS

Devotional Series

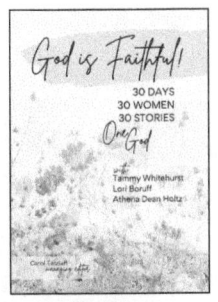

We Get You • *30-Day Devotional* | Compilation
ISBN soft 978-1-951350-185 • $14.99

Trusting God • *31-Day Devotional* | Compilation
ISBN soft 978-1-951350-833 • $14.99

God is Faithful • *31-Day Devotional* | Compilation
ISBN soft 978-1-64645-264-4 • $14.99

REDEMPTION
PRESS